This guide is dedicated to all the entrepreneurs and small business owners who are looking to make their mark in the ever-growing world of headphones and audio products. We understand the excitement, passion, and hard work that goes into starting a new venture, and we hope that this guide provides you with the valuable insights and knowledge you need to launch your headphone brand in India with confidence.

We would also like to dedicate this guide to the music lovers, audiophiles, and anyone who appreciates the power of sound and the impact that high-quality headphones can have on their lives. Your love for music and your support for new brands is what makes the audio industry such a dynamic and exciting place.

And finally, we dedicate this guide to the city of sound, Mumbai. A city that is renowned for its thriving music and film industries, and where the love for music and sound is deeply ingrained in the fabric of its culture. Mumbai, you are an inspiration to us all, and we hope that this guide helps to unleash the potential of the city's entrepreneurs and audio enthusiasts.

We hope that you find this guide useful and informative, and that it helps you to achieve the success that you are looking for in the world of headphones and audio products. Happy Launching!

LAUNCH YOUR HEADPHONE BRAND IN INDIA: THE ULTIMATE GUIDE

TUSHAR RAJ

Contents

Foreword

Welcome to "Launch Your Headphone Brand in India: The Ultimate Guide"!

In a world that is constantly evolving and adapting to new technology, the demand for quality headphones has never been higher. With India being one of the fastest-growing markets in the world, launching a headphone brand in this country has the potential to be a truly rewarding experience.

However, starting a business is never easy, and the challenges faced in the Indian market can be unique and overwhelming. That's where this guide comes in - to help you navigate the process of launching your headphone brand in India with confidence and success.

From market research and brand positioning, to product design and marketing strategies, this guide covers all the key aspects of launching a successful headphone brand in India. Whether you're a seasoned entrepreneur or just starting out, the insights and advice shared in this guide will provide valuable guidance on your journey to success.

So, let's dive in and take the first step towards realizing your dream of launching a successful headphone brand in India!

Preface

Dear reader,

Welcome to "Launch Your Headphone Brand in India: The Ultimate Guide". We are thrilled to have you with us on this exciting journey to help you successfully launch your headphone brand in India.

India is one of the fastest-growing economies in the world, making it a prime location for launching a new brand. However, with the increasing competition in the market, it can be challenging to establish your brand and make a lasting impact. That's where this guide comes in.

Our team of experts has worked hard to bring you a comprehensive guide to launching a headphone brand in India. From market research to product development and branding strategies, we've got you covered. Whether you're a seasoned entrepreneur or just starting out, this guide will provide you with valuable insights and actionable steps to help you make a smooth launch.

So sit back, relax, and let us take you through the process of launching your headphone brand in India. By the end of this guide, you'll have the knowledge and confidence to take on the market and succeed.

Thank you for choosing "Launch Your Headphone Brand in India: The Ultimate Guide". We wish you all the best in your entrepreneurial endeavors.

Best regards,

The Team at Launch Your Headphone Brand in India: The Ultimate Guide.

Acknowledgements

Writing a book is never a one-person task and this book is no exception. We would like to take this opportunity to extend our heartfelt gratitude to all the individuals and organizations who have supported us throughout the journey of writing this book.

Firstly, we would like to thank our families for their unwavering support, encouragement, and understanding during the long hours we spent writing and editing this book. Your love and support have been a source of motivation and inspiration for us.

We would also like to express our appreciation to the headphone industry experts who shared their valuable insights and knowledge with us. Your contributions have enriched the content of this book and provided us with a comprehensive understanding of the Indian headphone market.

We would like to extend our thanks to our publishers for their support and guidance in bringing this book to fruition. We are grateful for their belief in our work and for providing us with the resources to make it a success.

Finally, we would like to thank our readers for choosing this book. We hope that you will find it informative and helpful in launching your headphone brand in India. We look forward to hearing about your success stories and growth in the industry.

Thank you, once again, to all those who have made this book possible. Your support and contributions have been invaluable.

Prologue

Are you ready to take the Indian market by storm with your brand new headphones? Then, you've come to the right place! This guide is designed to give you a comprehensive and step-by-step approach to launching your headphone brand in India.

India is a rapidly growing market with an ever-increasing demand for consumer electronics. It presents a massive opportunity for businesses looking to establish themselves in the market. With the right strategies in place, your headphone brand can be the next big thing in India.

In this guide, we will cover everything from market research to product design, marketing strategies, and more. Whether you're starting from scratch or already have a brand established, this guide will provide you with the necessary information and insights to successfully launch your headphones in India.

We understand that launching a brand in a new market can be overwhelming, but with this guide, you'll have a solid plan of action to follow. So buckle up, grab a cup of chai, and let's get started on your journey to launching your headphone brand in India!

Author Info

Tushar Raj

ONE

INTRODUCTION

Welcome to the exciting world of launching your headphone brand in India! Before we dive into the nitty-gritty of how to launch your brand, let's take a moment to understand the Indian consumer electronics market and why it's the perfect place to launch your headphones.

A. Overview of the Indian Consumer Electronics Market

The Indian consumer electronics market has been growing rapidly in recent years and is expected to continue its growth trajectory in the coming years. According to a report by Market Research Future, the Indian consumer electronics market is expected to reach USD 400 billion by 2026. With an ever-increasing middle class, rising disposable income, and the rapid spread of technology, the demand for consumer electronics, including headphones, is on the rise in India.

B. Importance of Market Research

Before launching your headphones in India, it's important to conduct market research to gain insights into the Indian market and your target audience. Market research will help you understand the needs and preferences of your target audience, as well as the competitive landscape. This information will inform your product design, marketing strategy, and sales approach, ensuring that your headphones are positioned to meet the needs of the Indian market.

C. Understanding Your Target Audience

Knowing your target audience is crucial for the success of your headphone brand in India. Consider factors such as age, gender, income, and lifestyle when defining your target audience. This information will help you create a product that appeals to their needs and preferences and develop a marketing strategy that resonates with them.

In conclusion, understanding the Indian consumer electronics market and your target audience is the foundation of a successful headphone launch in India. With this knowledge, you'll be well on your way to launching a successful brand and capturing a piece of the Indian market.

TWO

PRODUCT DESIGN AND DEVELOPMENT

Now that you have a solid understanding of the Indian consumer electronics market and your target audience, it's time to dive into the heart of your launch plan: product design and development.

A. Choosing the Right Features for the Indian Market

When it comes to designing your headphones, it's important to keep the Indian market in mind. What features are most important to your target audience? What are their pain points and what solutions can you offer? Conducting market research will give you valuable insights into the needs and preferences of your target audience.

B. Packaging and Branding for the Indian Market

In addition to the features of your headphones, it's important to consider the packaging and branding. Packaging should be visually appealing and easy to open, while also providing adequate protection during shipping.

Consider using colors and imagery that resonate with the Indian market, while also staying true to your brand's identity.

Branding is also an important factor in the Indian market. A strong brand can help you stand out in a crowded market, build trust with your target audience, and establish a loyal customer base. Make sure your brand reflects the values and personality of your company, and consider using cultural references or imagery that will resonate with the Indian market.

C. Testing and Quality Assurance

Once your headphones are designed, it's time to put them through rigorous testing to ensure they meet high quality standards. This includes functionality testing, durability testing, and performance testing. You should also consider getting your headphones certified by a reputable third-party organization.

By conducting thorough testing and quality assurance, you'll be able to identify any potential issues and make any necessary changes before launching your headphones in India. This will also give you peace of mind knowing that your headphones meet high quality standards and will perform well for your target audience.

In conclusion, product design and development is a critical step in launching your headphones in India. By focusing on the needs and preferences of the Indian market, developing a strong brand, and conducting thorough testing and quality assurance, you'll be well on your way to success.

THREE

Marketing and Sales Strategy

Marketing and sales are critical components of any successful business, and launching a headphone brand in India is no exception. In this chapter, we'll explore various marketing and sales strategies that you can use to get your brand noticed and drive sales. Let's get started!

A. Developing a Marketing Plan

Before you start launching your headphone brand, it's important to develop a comprehensive marketing plan. Your marketing plan should outline your target audience, your marketing budget, and your marketing objectives. It should also detail the tactics you'll use to reach your target audience, including advertising, promotions, public relations, and events.

When developing your marketing plan, it's crucial to understand the Indian market and your target audience. For example, if your target audience is primarily made up of young professionals, you might want to focus your marketing efforts on social media and digital advertising. If your target audience is more traditional, you may want to focus on print and outdoor advertising.

B. Creating a Strong Online Presence

In today's digital age, it's crucial to have a strong online presence. In India, the majority of consumers research products online before making a purchase, so having a well-designed website and strong social media presence can make a big difference in your sales.

Make sure your website is user-friendly, visually appealing, and easy to navigate. Your website should also provide detailed information about your headphones, including specifications, pricing, and a store locator.

In addition to your website, you should also have a presence on popular social media platforms like Facebook, Instagram, and Twitter. Use these platforms to engage with your audience, promote your headphones, and build brand awareness.

C. Building Relationships with Retailers and Distributors

Building relationships with retailers and distributors is crucial for your success in the Indian market. Retailers and distributors can help you get your headphones in front of consumers, increase your visibility, and drive sales.

When selecting retailers and distributors, look for those that have a strong reputation, a proven track record of success, and a good understanding of the Indian market. It's also important to have a clear agreement in place that outlines your expectations and obligations.

D. Utilizing Influencer Marketing and Word of Mouth

Influencer marketing and word of mouth can be highly effective marketing tactics in India. Influencer marketing involves partnering with popular bloggers, social media influencers, or celebrities to promote your headphones. Word of mouth, on the other hand, involves encouraging your customers to spread the word about your headphones to their friends and family.

When using influencer marketing, it's important to choose influencers that align with your brand values and have a large and engaged following. When encouraging word of mouth, consider offering incentives or rewards to customers who refer friends and family to your brand.

In conclusion, a comprehensive marketing and sales strategy is critical to the success of your headphone brand in India. From developing a marketing plan to building relationships with retailers and distributors, there are many tactics you can use to reach your target audience and drive sales. With a well-thought-out plan in place, you'll be well on your way to launching a successful headphone brand in India.

FOUR

LEGAL AND REGULATORY CONSIDERATIONS

Starting a business in India can be a complex process, but it's important to ensure that you're following all the necessary legal and regulatory requirements. In this chapter, we'll cover some of the key considerations that you'll need to keep in mind as you launch your headphone brand in India.

A. Obtaining Required Licenses and Permits

Before you can start selling your headphones in India, you'll need to obtain any necessary licenses and permits. This will depend on the type of business you're operating, as well as the state or territory in which you'll be selling your products. You may need to register your business with the Registrar of Companies (ROC), obtain a tax identification number (TIN), and register for VAT or GST, among other things.

B. Understanding Tax and Import Regulations

In addition to obtaining the necessary licenses and permits, you'll also need to understand the tax and import regulations that apply to your business. For example, you may need to pay customs duties and taxes when importing components or materials for your headphones. You'll also need to understand the tax implications of selling your headphones in India, such as VAT or GST, and ensure that you're staying compliant with these regulations.

C. Protecting Your Intellectual Property

Finally, it's important to protect your intellectual property, such as your brand name, logo, and design, in India. This may involve registering your trademark in India and ensuring that your products are properly labeled and packaged to avoid any confusion or infringement.

In conclusion, following the legal and regulatory requirements for launching your headphone brand in India may seem overwhelming, but it's essential to ensure the success and longevity of your business. It's always a good idea to consult with a lawyer or legal advisor to ensure that you're following the correct procedures and meeting all of your obligations.

Don't let legal and regulatory considerations dampen your excitement for launching your headphone brand in India. With the right preparation and guidance, you'll be able to navigate these requirements with ease and focus on growing your business in the Indian market.

FIVE

OPERATIONS AND LOGISTICS

Congratulations! You're almost there. By now, you've done your market research, designed and developed your headphones, and planned your marketing and sales strategy. The next step is to get your headphones from your manufacturing facility to the hands of your customers. That's where operations and logistics come in.

A. Sourcing Components and Materials

Sourcing the right components and materials is critical to the success of your headphone brand. You want to make sure that you're getting the best quality materials at the right price. Start by researching suppliers in India and abroad. Consider factors such as cost, quality, delivery time, and reliability. Be sure to compare multiple suppliers and get quotes from each before making a decision.

B. Warehouse and Inventory Management

Once you have your components and materials, it's time to store them in a warehouse. This will give you the space you need to store your products until they're ready to be shipped to customers. You'll also want to implement an inventory management system that will help you keep track of your stock levels and reorder materials when necessary.

C. Shipping and Delivery Solutions

Finally, it's time to get your headphones to your customers. You'll need to decide on the best shipping and delivery solutions for your business. There are several options to choose from, including standard ground shipping, expedited shipping, and even same-day delivery. You'll also want to consider shipping costs and delivery times to ensure that you're providing the best possible customer experience.

In conclusion, operations and logistics are critical to the success of your headphone brand in India. By sourcing the right components and materials, implementing a warehouse and inventory management system, and choosing the best shipping and delivery solutions, you'll be able to get your headphones to your customers quickly and efficiently. With these key steps in place, you'll be well on your way to launching your headphone brand in India!

SIX

CONCLUSION

Congratulations, you've made it to the end of this guide! By now, you should have a solid understanding of the steps involved in launching your headphone brand in India. From market research to product design, marketing strategies, legal and regulatory considerations, and operations and logistics, we've covered it all.

Key Takeaways

1. India is a rapidly growing market with a high demand for consumer electronics.

2. Market research is crucial for understanding your target audience and the competition.

3. Product design, packaging, and branding should be tailored to the Indian market.

4. Building a strong online presence and utilizing influencer marketing can be effective marketing strategies.

5. Obtaining necessary licenses and permits, and understanding tax and import regulations are important legal and regulatory considerations.

6. Sourcing components and materials, and managing warehouse and inventory are important aspects of operations and logistics.

The Future of the Indian Consumer Electronics Market

The future of the Indian consumer electronics market looks promising, with increasing demand for a variety of products, including headphones. With the right strategies in place, your headphone brand can establish itself in the market and thrive.

Final Thoughts and Next Steps

By following the steps outlined in this guide, you're well on your way to launching a successful headphone brand in India. Remember to always keep market trends and your target audience in mind as you make decisions, and don't be afraid to adapt and pivot as needed.

The next step is to start putting your plan into action! From conducting market research to developing a marketing plan, every step is important in ensuring the success of your launch. So, get out there and make it happen!

We hope this guide has been helpful in your journey to launching your headphone brand in India. Best of luck, and here's to your success!

Sample Marketing Plan Outline

As you launch your headphone brand in India, it's crucial to have a solid marketing plan in place. This plan should be a comprehensive document that outlines your goals, target audience, budget, and strategies for promoting and selling your products.

Here's a sample outline for a marketing plan for your headphone brand in India:

I. Executive Summary

A. Overview of your headphone brand

B. Marketing goals and objectives

C. Target audience and customer segments

D. Budget and the timeline for marketing activities

II. Market Research and Analysis

A. Overview of the Indian consumer electronics market

B. Competitor analysis

C. Understanding your target audience and customer segments

III. Product Positioning and Branding

A. Unique selling proposition (USP)

B. Packaging and product design

C. Brand identity and messaging

IV. Marketing and Promotion Strategies

A. Online marketing and advertising

B. Influencer marketing and word of mouth

C. Retail partnerships and distribution channels

D. Trade shows and events

V. Sales and Distribution Strategies

A. Retail partnerships and distribution channels

B. E-commerce and online sales

C. Sales and marketing materials (e.g. brochures, flyers)

VI. Budget and Timeline

A. Allocation of budget for marketing activities

B. Timeline for marketing activities and milestones

VII. Evaluation and Adjustment

A. Measuring the success of your marketing efforts

B. Adjusting your strategies as needed

Your marketing plan should be a living document that you continually update and adjust based on the success of your marketing activities. It should be a roadmap for your marketing efforts and will help you stay on track as you work to build awareness and drive sales for your headphone brand in India.

By following this outline, you'll be well on your way to creating a comprehensive marketing plan for your headphone brand in India. With a solid plan in place, you'll be able to effectively promote and sell your products, and build a successful brand in the Indian market.

Sample Budget Template For Launching A Headphone Brand

When launching a new business, it's important to have a clear understanding of the costs involved. This will help you to make informed decisions and ensure that you have enough funding to get your brand off the ground. In this section, we'll provide you with a sample budget template for launching a headphone brand in India.

Please note that this is a sample budget and may not reflect the exact costs for your specific launch. Your actual costs will depend on several factors, including the size of your launch, the number of headphones you plan to manufacture, and the marketing and advertising strategies you choose to pursue.

Here's a breakdown of the costs you might expect to incur when launching your headphone brand in India:

A. Product Development and Design

1. Product design and prototyping: INR 100,000 - 200,000

2. Tooling and manufacturing setup: INR 250,000 - 500,000

3. Product testing and quality assurance: INR 50,000 - 100,000

B. Marketing and Sales

1. Website design and development: INR 50,000 - 100,000

2. Influencer marketing and brand ambassadors: INR 100,000 - 200,000

3. Advertising and promotion: INR 200,000 - 500,000

4. Sales and distribution expenses: INR 500,000 - 1,000,000

C. Legal and Regulatory

1. Business registration and licenses: INR 10,000 - 50,000

2. Intellectual property protection: INR 50,000 - 100,000

3. Legal and tax consulting: INR 100,000 - 200,000

D. Operations and Logistics

1. Warehouse and storage: INR 50,000 - 100,000

2. Shipping and delivery: INR 200,000 - 500,000

3. Inventory management: INR 100,000 - 200,000

E. Miscellaneous

1. Professional services (e.g. accounting, consulting): INR 50,000 - 100,000

2. Miscellaneous expenses (e.g. office supplies, travel): INR 50,000 - 100,000

* Total Estimated Cost: INR 2,000,000 - 4,000,000

It's important to remember that this is just a sample budget and that your actual costs may be higher or lower depending on your specific launch. To create a more accurate budget for your launch, it's recommended that you work with a financial advisor or business consultant. They can help you to identify potential costs and make sure that you have a solid plan in place for funding your launch.

With a solid budget in place, you'll be well on your way to launching your headphone brand in India. Good luck!

Notes